WALKING ON EGGSHELLS

WALKING
ON
EGGSHELLS

PRACTICAL COUNSEL FOR WOMEN
IN OR LEAVING A VIOLENT RELATIONSHIP

by
DR. BRIAN OGAWA

VOLCANO
· PRESS ·

Volcano, California

Dedicated to Brent and Brooke

WALKING ON EGGSHELLS Copyright © 1989, 1992 and 1996 by Dr. Brian Ogawa

First editions of WALKING ON EGGSHELLS published in 1989 and 1992 by the Victim/Witness Assistance Program, Department of the Prosecuting Attorney, County of Maui, Wailuku, Hawaii.

Library of Congress Cataloging-in-Publication Data

Ogawa, Brian K.
    Walking on eggshells : practical counsel for women in or leaving a violent
relationship / written by Brian Ogawa.
       p.   cm.
    Originally published: Wailuku, Hawaii : Victim/Witness Assistance Program, Dept.
of the Prosecuting Attorney, County of Maui, © 1989.
    ISBN 1-884244-11-4
    1. Abused wives—Counseling of. 2. Abused women—Counseling of.
I. Title.
HV1444.O38   1996
362.82'9286—dc20   95-52905
                                                  CIP

Text and cover concept by Wagstaff Design, Maui, Hawaii
Composition by Jeff Brandenburg, ImageComp
Production by David Charlsen & Others

The case histories in this book are authentic, but the names have been changed to protect the privacy of the subjects.

To order additional copies of WALKING ON EGGSHELLS, please send $8.95. For postage and handling, add $4.50 for the first book and $1.00 for each additional book. California residents only add appropriate sales tax. Contact Volcano Press for quantity discount rates, and for a free current catalog.

Volcano Press, Inc. P.O. Box 20, Volcano, CA 95689.
Web address: http://www.volcanopress.com. Email: sales@volcanopress.com.

FOR ORDERS ONLY: (800) 879-9636 • FAX: (209) 296-4995

Printed in the United States of America

03 02   10 9 8 7 6 5 4 3

CONTENTS

FOREWORD

As you read this book, you will share the experiences of other women who have suffered violence in their relationships with men. You will learn some basic principles to guide you in changing your personal situation. Only you can determine what gives you meaning and purpose in life, and what should be judged as failure or success in your relationship. This book, however, offers you a helpful understanding of the nature of violent relationships, encouragement to no longer submit to abuse, and a plan for the future.

INTRODUCTION

Ann was the woman who first described to me that her home life was like "walking on eggshells." When she met her husband, Richard, he was attentive and polite. She was initially drawn to him because he was well-educated, articulate, and ambitious. Soon after their marriage, however, Richard assumed license to correct her at every opportunity. As Ann remembers:

> *There wasn't a definite beginning to the eggshell feeling. It started as a simple uneasiness that I just was not quite good enough to do a certain task. He let me know how his experience and knowledge were so much more extensive and varied, and that he was, without a doubt, the better authority on any given subject.*

Richard's program of "correction" became increasingly rigid and insulting. If Ann did not iron his shirts perfectly, for example, he would crumple them and throw them on the floor. If she was late, even five minutes, for any dinner that he had prepared, he would discard it in the sink, saying that it was ruined.

Outbursts of physical violence eventually followed. Slaps and shoves became mixed with threats and obscenities.

> *Covering the ground with eggshells was a slow process. As time went on, it was obvious that I could not second-guess or control every item in life so as to not upset this man. Walking on eggshells is the closest I can come to explaining the sense of impending dread, fear of being demeaned, wanting somehow to carve peaceful moments from days of anxiety.*

Ann did finally leave her husband. She escaped before she was seriously injured and before she completely lost her sense of herself as a person. Richard manipulated the outcome of the divorce proceedings so that he obtained most of their material possessions and financial assets. These mattered relatively little to Ann. She had lived with fear and uncertainty too long. Her body had been under constant stress and her emotions were frayed from being always "on call" to her husband. He had wanted her to believe that she was negatively affecting *his* life by her "stupidity." She at last realized that it was *her* life which was, in fact, being methodically destroyed.

Ann's experience is sadly descriptive of that of many women. The cover illustration for this book of a feather floating just above cracked eggshells is a fitting symbol for a woman who is in a precarious place in her relationship. A feather carries little weight, substance, or influence. It is at the mercy and whim of the forces brought to bear against it. In the same manner, the opinions and needs of a woman in a violent relationship are not taken seriously by the abuser. Her wishes are trivial compared to his own neediness to exercise power and control.

If you are in such a relationship, you are forced to "walk lightly," hesitating at every step. It is impossible not to break the eggshells strewn before you. No matter how careful you are, the conditions and rules that he sets before you cannot be met except by the total surrender of your will. Taking a stand, defending a position, and moving too slowly or too independently are not permitted or safe. As a woman, your role in a relationship where violence occurs is reduced to one of *submission*.

The feather, however, does float *over* the cracked eggshells. This is a testimony to those women who have not surrendered. You are doing your best to cope and survive daily.

There are times when your self-perception is clouded. Dreams of security, family, and love have faded. Self-doubts enter your mind regarding the causes of what went wrong. But whether you commit to continue efforts to improve the relationship or recognize that it is time to leave, these decisions indicate the integrity of your own person.

Every woman has the right to make choices in her life. Although the abuser attempts to severely restrict these choices, you can act, as long as there is a whisper of hope or a kernel of resolve within you. The feather has characteristics which enable it to remain aloft. You also have qualities which define you as much more than just an abused woman.

1 RELATIONSHIPS
IN A WOMAN'S LIFE

Relationships are the cradle of the most meaningful experiences in our lives. From birth, through childhood and adolescence, in marriage and parenthood, culminating in our senior years, the journey of life is filled with challenges. Our quest for happiness and harmony and love, though never smooth, is the very nature and inspiration of our being.

BOYS HAVE MORE PRIVILEGES THAN GIRLS

The success of our relationships is dependent upon a mixture of social influence, learned behavior, personal character, good fortune, and discernment. During our childhood, patterns of these relationships are modeled by our parents and other important adults. Although we are not photocopies of their precise words and actions, these adults play an influence in how we perceive and value relationships.

One of the first things Marla, for example, remembers learning about relationships is that if you were a boy, you had more privileges. Boys were allowed to do more than girls. They didn't have to work harder to gain this position; it was simply a matter of gender. Marla therefore tried to become more boy-like. She dressed, played games, and climbed trees as a tomboy. As she grew older, the tomboy notion fell away:

I began to see other ways in which women needed to act and react to get what they wanted. I watched my mother get angry at my father for making "stupid" decisions. I was convinced that my mother was more intelligent and that my father was ineffectual. Communication was mostly surface conversation and arguments. There was no love demonstrated between the two. My aunts and uncles were the same. The women had the brains but could not act; the men had the power but little intelligence. Power always won out in the end.

Society—in its political, educational and religious institutions, community standards, and media representations—overlays our childhood influences and training. Unfortunately, throughout history and across cultures, women have generally occupied a subservient position. Not only do boys have more privileges than girls, but men have more rights than women. This message contributes each day to unknown numbers of women being battered in their homes by their husbands, brutalized by their boyfriends, or murdered by partners. The restraints against violence toward women that have existed have usually been minimal, poorly enforced, or lacking in penalties. Women in abusive relationships may thus have awareness that they are in deep trouble but may not know that there are alternatives.

> *Standing in the doorway to my office, my friend said to me, "Something has got to change." I tried wiping the tears from my already swollen eyes and just looked back at her until she looked downward, closed the door lightly, and walked away. I knew something was terribly wrong, yet how was I supposed to know what was right? My parents had fought and they stayed together. Everybody I knew fought but stuck it out. I had described to another girlfriend what I had come to think of as one of the more mild fights. She reacted much stronger than I expected. She insisted, "You do know that you do not have to put up with that in a relationship, don't you?" I said, "Of course." Truthfully, I wasn't sure.*

BASHO, TENNYSON, AND O'KEEFFE

Basho was a Japanese poet of the 17th century. He is known for a *haiku* (17-syllable poem), which, translated into English, reads:

> *When I look carefully*
> *I see the* nazuna *blooming*
> *by the hedge!*

Apparently, while walking a country path, Basho noticed something rather neglected by the hedge. He approached to find a wild plant in bloom. A strong feeling stirred within him. In a flower inconspicuous to other passersby, Basho marveled at every petal and experienced the deepest mystery of life. It was as if the flower saw Basho as Basho saw the flower! There was a *oneness* established between them.

In contrast, the English poet Tennyson expresses the theme of *dominance* in this poem:

> *Flower in the crannied wall,*
> *I pluck you out of the crannies;*
> *Hold you here, root and all, in my hand.*
> *Little flower—but if I could understand*
> *What you are, root and all, and all in all,*
> *I should know what God and man is.*

Tennyson tore the flower from the place where it grew. The flower, separated from the ground where it belonged, soon withered and died. Tennyson had little regard for the flower other than for the purpose that it served for him.

Georgia O'Keeffe was a celebrated American artist, heralded for her paintings of flowers drawn in large and bold strokes. She described her art in this way:

> *A flower is relatively small. . . . You put out your hand to touch the flower—lean forward to smell it—maybe touch it with your lips almost without thinking—or give it to someone to please them. Still—in a way—nobody sees a flower—really—it is so small—we haven't time—and to see takes time like to have a friend takes time. . . . So I said to myself—I'll paint what I see—what the flower is to me but I'll paint it big and they will be surprised into taking time to look at it.*
> *("About Myself," 1939)*

O'Keeffe leads us to see what we would otherwise miss. She elicits and captures our attention with her bright and colorful renderings.

Basho, Tennyson, and O'Keeffe provide us with a means of evaluating and understanding relationships. Basho communicates gentleness and admiration. He did not even touch the *nazuna* but found contentment and inspiration in its presence. Tennyson exemplifies the need to possess and control. The flower became *his* property, to have for *his* benefit. O'Keeffe allows us to see the flower *as a flower* with all of its radiance and worth. The flower brings enjoyment but not at the cost of its own identity.

APPRECIATION AND RESPECT

For some men, the life canvas of women is painted with pale and weak brush strokes. These men have not learned that relationships cannot exist serving the advantage of one person over the other. Relationships flourish when there is appreciation and respect for the strengths and abilities of each person.

Tennyson forfeited closeness for the sake of selfish intent. Basho humbly gazed upon the *nazuna* and experienced life's essence. O'Keeffe highlighted the true qualities of a flower in dramatic hues. Women deserve the same acknowledgment as exemplified by Basho and O'Keeffe.

> *I want a relationship where I have pleasure being in his company. I don't want to be ignored but I don't want to be smothered.*

A man, however, who abuses a woman views her as an available and easy *object* of his anger, frustration, and insecurities. The woman is "at fault" and must be ruled and punished. The plausibility of a relationship is shattered under these circumstances. A woman who is a "target" is absorbed with dodging, hiding, avoiding, appeasing. Her self-respect is in jeopardy and the only "respect" likely to evolve is one that is demanded and extorted by the abuser.

MORITA PRINCIPLES

Shoma Morita was a Tokyo psychiatrist and university professor (1874–1938), who made keen observations about suffering and summarized these in simple truths. He was particularly interested in the difficulties people experienced in relationships, their obsessions, fears, and anxieties.

Morita illustrated several of his principles by the analogy of the "flowing river." The conduct of a person's life resembles that of a river. The river flows from a mountain source and encounters many obstacles as it travels toward its destination of the far-off sea. Along its way, the river finds the most direct course of least resistance. The river does not stop at each obstruction and question why it is present. It does not attempt to remove every hindrance from the riverbed before it can proceed. The river is affected by what it meets: the rocks are sharp and the fallen trees are formidable. These, however, do not deter the river from keeping to its appointed course.

In the same manner, Morita argued that our lives have a natural flow when we are motivated by a strong desire to live well and are guided by clear purposes. This flow is not always smooth and uninterrupted. But if we allow adversities to defeat us or give up in the face of hardships, we eddy like a side current of the river. There, we stagnate on the periphery of life.

The most meaningful lifeway, therefore, according to Morita, is (1) to be in touch with your feelings about what you are experiencing and to accept them as they are without being overwhelmed or controlled by them; (2) to concentrate on whatever specific task most obviously needs to be completed *now;* and (3) to set about changing your situation for the better in every constructive and responsible way open to you. In the following chapters, these principles will be more fully explained in terms of surviving and recovering from abusive relationships.

2 DISGUISED EMOTIONS

Noh masks are a favorite means for stage actors in Japan to quickly portray different emotions, facial expressions, and several characters without cumbersome and elaborate wardrobe and makeup changes. Easily worn or held in front of the actor's face, these light wooden masks often symbolize generalized emotions such as sadness or cheerfulness. Experienced Japanese actors are adept at switching from one mask to another almost by ritual. A Noh drama is a work of art and precision.

MASKS WE WEAR

Many of us wear masks in our daily lives. We become skilled at revealing or not revealing how we feel, depending upon the surroundings in which we find ourselves. There are times when our true feelings about a person, a certain subject, or what we are experiencing are not expressed to others. It may be rude, inappropriate, embarrassing, or too personal to share what we are actually feeling.

Women in violent relationships encounter the added risk of being ridiculed, assaulted, and injured by the men in their lives for showing what they are feeling. As one woman related:

> *I grew up thinking that emotions were something that you did not share with others—you took them back to your room and closed the door. When I was married I had very strong emotions. They were so strong that I couldn't easily just take them back to "my room." I had feelings of rage at how he was mistreating me, but I found it safer not to express them—instead I would withdraw. In fact, I became very good at gauging when a rampage was about to begin and I would simply leave the house, away from all noise, unpleasantness, and conflict. Frequently, I would just fall asleep.*

There were times, nevertheless, when her husband would not permit her to leave the house. He would stand by the doorway and block her exit or take away her car keys. If she was asleep, he would roughly shake her to gain her attention. As a result, she became even more passive, enduring whatever she needed to in order to be left alone once again.

One day, however, she walked into their bedroom to discover that he had torn a hole in her hand-embroidered jewelry case. She had on other occasions returned home to find her clothes ripped to shreds and other personal belongings broken. But this time, she exploded. As he tried to find something else to damage, she tried to stop him. He pushed her aside but she pushed him back. They were both startled by her response. She then pounded his chest with her hands, screaming words of intense anger and hurt. Her husband's reaction to this outpouring shocked and sickened her. In his face she saw a smile of contempt and victory. "That's it!" he said. "Let it out, let it all come out!" By unleashing her emotions, she provided him with further "evidence" that she was "crazy," and therefore whatever he did to her and her possessions was "for her own good."

The masks we wear to hide our emotions also are used to protect those areas of our lives that take on heightened importance because of the violence. For example, your friends may know your true situation and your feelings about it. But you may also disguise your emotions from others in order for them to continue seeing you in a favorable light.

> *I did not want to be the picture of a pitiful woman in my friends' eyes. I had enough of that at home. On the contrary, most of my friends and people I worked with saw me as a capable and outgoing person. Their view of me actually bolstered me much of the time, for the view I had of myself was much worse.*

MISLABELING EMOTIONS

We often label and separate emotions as being either good or bad, because of how we feel when we are experiencing them or because they are associated with certain events. Fear, anxiety, sadness, for example, are frequently considered negative emotions, while courage, trust, happiness are positive ones. We then *mistakenly* measure the quality of our lives by how we feel at any given time.

Moreover, having been denied in a violent relationship the right to feel much of anything, it becomes easier to prefer a sense of numbness.

> *As I look back, I remember being in such excruciating emotional pain, I thought that I would not survive until the next day. I was living day to day, awaiting and trying to create peaceful moments so that I could say my life was okay.*

Emotions, however, are essentially our *natural responses* to what is occurring in our lives. The death of a loved one brings tremendous feelings of loss. Danger instills fear. Success generates confidence. Since life events are ever-changing, our emotions correspondingly change "like the Japanese autumn sky." You may generalize, for example, that you have been feeling depressed all week, but if you were to list each and every emotion that you felt during that week, you would find that you had actually experienced a wide variety and intensity of emotions. For emotions naturally mushroom within us, wane, and disappear, if we are attending and responding to what life is continuously bringing to us.

Emotions, in this way, are like *signposts*. Emotions that regularly persist alert you to compare what you are experiencing to the purposes you have identified for your life. They may be warning you to detour from the direction you are going. They may be telling you that something is not to your benefit. Distress, for example, is not a pleasant feeling, but it tells you that what you feel distressed about is contrary to what you desire in life.

In other words, you do not govern your emotions. No matter how strong your preference to feel a certain way, that does not guarantee you will experience that feeling. You may pledge to feel only jovial the entire day, but other emotions will inevitably creep in and out. You should not therefore dictate your life by what you are feeling, because you would then live without any consistency. The most productive manner of living is to "do what needs to be done," despite what you are feeling at any particular moment.

ACCEPTANCE

If emotions are naturally related to what you are experiencing, if they are not something over which you exercise direct control, and if they offer some guidance for your life, then the most advantageous approach to whatever you are feeling is acceptance. This means that there is no right or wrong to what you are feeling. There is no stigma or self-judgment for feeling a certain way. You have the *freedom to feel* whatever feelings arise, because something over which you have no control is something for which you also have no responsibility. You are only responsible for how constructively you live your life. It is the integrity of your actions, not the state of your emotions, that attests to your character.

As a woman in an abusive relationship, you may *feel* helpless, but that does not mean that you *are* helpless. He may impose cruel boundaries encircling what you can undertake. Feeling helpless, however, is not an excuse for neglecting to act upon the opportunities which may be present.

Acceptance of *whatever* you are feeling, therefore, does not mean resigning yourself to feelings of misery in a miserable situation. It means that "feeling better" is given less priority than "living better." All your energies should be directed toward what is controllable in your life rather than what is not controllable. You do not control his behavior and you do not control what you feel. You do, with few exceptions, control your own actions.

Some women are tempted to dull their pain through alcohol and sedatives. Some seek to distract themselves by "keeping busy," rummaging for things to occupy their minds and fill their time. These tactics fail because solutions to a violent relationship do not come from avoidance, retreat, or wishful thinking.

> *I would confide sometimes in a few, close friends. As I told them of the latest, awful event, they would comfort me or tell me flat out to leave him. I had convinced them that the man I was living with was cruel and manipulative. The very next day, however, if he was nice and kind to me, I would believe that he was wonderful and the "bad times" had passed. When my friends would then refer to him as a "jerk," I would be offended. I needed them to listen when things were going bad but resented them for bringing up any "history."*

Acceptance *begins* with admitting that you are a victim of abuse and not denying or minimizing what you are feeling. Acceptance *broadens* as you confess what can and cannot change in the relationship. Acceptance is *complete* when you assume the risk and responsibility to take some course of action despite feeling inadequate, nervous, or timid. To try to suppress such feelings without addressing the circumstances to which they are connected, leads to a greater sense of help-lessness. To instead make some effort to change your circum-stances establishes the greater likelihood that you will feel stronger. Periodically, you will feel uncertain. But each step, no matter how small, provides the footing for continued growth.

3 CREATING CLARITY IN YOUR LIFE

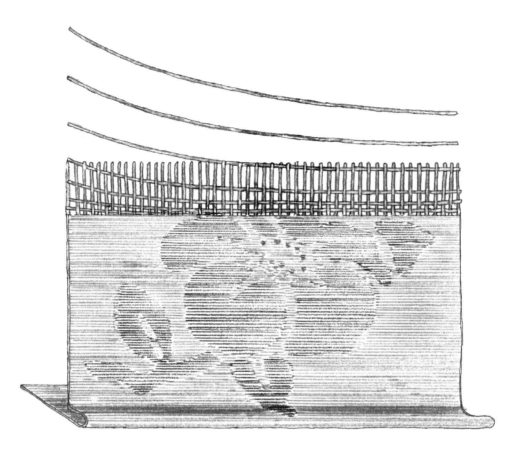

When she was a young girl growing up in a small town, Mary would visit with her mother, an elderly woman who made her living by weaving cloth rugs on a loom in her home. Mary remembered vividly the piles of rags and strands of fabric of every imaginable kind on the floor by this woman's loom. Most of the material was brought by neighbors in partial exchange for the finished product. Good cloth such as silk was gathered with old towels and discarded shirts and dresses. Somehow, as if by magic (in the young girl's eyes), a kitchen rug of wonderful design would appear! These rugs adorned the homes of many townspeople.

WEAVING LIFE'S FABRIC

Events, persons, and places create the fabric of your life. At any stage, the present fabric is the work of weaving and re-weaving of many threads, of varying colors and textures. The design of the fabric, at certain moments, may seem more a tangled web than a wearable or usable cloth. Through careful and patient reworking, however, taking bits and pieces and learning from old patterns, you can create an identifiable and new design for your life.

Some tasks are slow and painstaking, producing something worthwhile only after an arduous process. Perhaps miracles do happen, but it is usually what we do each moment that is the fundamental material for our lives. Clarity, in other words, does not come from wishing we knew what to do as much as *doing well what we already know must be done.*

You have at least some vision of what you desire in life. Even if it is just wishing that the violence would end, that is a beginning. Discovering what is beyond will only come after you start to actualize what is clearly now before you.

> *My life with him was a nightmare. He has beaten me until I have bled from my ears. He inflicted bruises over every part of my body. He used to take me for walks in the woods with the children and would blow up small trees with a shotgun. He would then turn the gun on us and threaten to blow our heads off if I reported him. I am not running anymore. I am tired of living this way.*

Linda took a fearful first step by contacting a woman's shelter. She then notified the police and eventually testified in court against her husband. She could not afford to wait to feel brave before fleeing. Her initial action needed to be firm and quick, based upon the best plan possible at that moment. She was thereafter more prepared to chart what she had to do next.

THE STORY

There are women who endure their abuse in silence. Their quiet suffering, however, does not mean that their minds and hearts are not filled to bursting with the need to be heard. There are also women who tell their stories to trusted friends repeatedly and often. It is a way of doing something in a situation in which there appears to be little else that can be done. These women do not fabricate or embellish their abuse. On the contrary, many women minimize that is happening to them or detach themselves as if the abuse were occurring to another person.

For Rachel, however, telling the story of her abuse became tiresome.

> *I was frustrated at listening to myself talk about how I was being mistreated by my husband again. My best friend Patti was patient but my story never changed and neither was my life changing. Talking helped but I was also reminded that I was still talking about the same thing over many years.*

Rachel also had been seeing her therapist twice a week for a year and a half. Each time she would describe some horrible occurrence in her life. One summer, she attended a wilderness camp for one week. She came back "calm, relaxed, and exuberant about life." The time away from her husband had made a remarkable difference. But ever so quickly, another battle ensued with him. She went to the next session with her therapist crying and relating yet another story about the most recent awful event. It was during that session that the therapist told her that there was no use to continue in treatment.

> *She saw me as too caught up in my situation to help myself. All the attention upon the hurt and pain in my relationship had prevented me from seeing that I just needed to end the suffering by getting away from my husband. Ironically, after years of entering therapies to receive help, what really made the difference was being told that this was our last session. I needed to stop telling my story and begin living my life.*

LIFE PRESERVERS

Shipwrecked survivors on the open sea depend upon their life preservers to avoid drowning from fatigue or injury. Any person, likewise, who is in crisis or under threat, clings to something or someone for safety. For one woman, her cats became essential to her coping:

> *My cats, three of them, were the objects of my caring and nurturing feelings during this time. I began to treat them as my children and tried my best to protect them through the bouts of yelling and screaming. I found solitude with them.*

Another woman found some peace in being alone in the library, reading books and browsing. Another would take late night drives to the harbor to watch sailing ships glide by. Yet another became immersed in the routines of her workplace. Her projects and assignments there helped her to temporarily feel that her problems were "a million miles away."

Always being confronted with violence or living under the fear of violence is beyond anyone's resources. Prolonged attachment and overdependence on anyone or anything as a way of not dealing directly with your situation can prevent, however, any clear focus on real solutions. It is as if the passing ships and nearby shores are not noticed because the life preserver itself fills your attention and is so tightly embraced. Being preoccupied with *just* surviving exacts a toll on your well-being.

REDIRECTION

Women who experience violence in their relationships are not truly passive. Your actions, however, may frequently be of a defensive nature. Since your actions can easily be criticized by your spouse or boyfriend as misbehavior, you may seek to improve your odds by tailoring your behavior to avoid his reaction.

Persons who stutter, for example, avoid certain words that give them difficulty. Similarly, abused women will sometimes try to avoid situations where violence may be triggered. This may mean "simplifying" the home environment by keeping the children quiet and out of the way, or by not inviting guests or relatives to visit.

Being on the defensive, ironically, increases the power that the abuser exerts over you. You can only create clarity in your life by beginning to redirect your attention away from his violence, away from repeating your story without change or resolution, and away from overreliance upon short-term and stopgap measures. This redirection occurs as you point the life preserver toward some destination and kick your feet to achieve some movement. Partially letting go of the life preserver, you start to paddle with one hand. Each stroke and kick represents practice and enables you to improve. Small efforts accumulate and build upon one another toward some result.

Assuming personal responsibility is an anchor in the midst of being so very much controlled by someone else. You are not responsible for how he mistreats you, even if he places the blame on you. You are, nevertheless, responsible for determining goals for your life and attempting those things necessary to reach them.

4 EACH MOMENT IS A NEW ONE

Doors are curious inventions. Unopened, they shut us off from what is on the other side. Opened, they present us with a choice to remain where we are or to pass through to what awaits us. If we choose to walk through the doorway, we can either shut the door behind us or leave it open. Doors therefore symbolize both barrier and invitation to experience something new.

DOORWAYS

Abusive men persuade and terrorize women to believe that there are no doorways in their lives. These men are the door-keepers. They construct their homes as if there are few windows from which to see the world outside. Some women therefore lose all perspective of themselves and their abilities, so that even the idea of an exit from the relationship appears inconceivable.

There are also many other women who recognize that it is time to leave the relationship and construct their own means of escape. This realization often causes feelings of loneliness and failure. There may even be several attempts to leave, which are abandoned because of self-doubts and the lingering hope that he might change.

> *There are supposed to be tough times in a relationship. I just needed to weather the storms. But the few good moments were not making up for all the hurt and countless unhappy times anymore. Why am I still with him after six years?*

SEARCHING FOR THE WHY'S

Susan knew in part why she had remained with her husband, Bill. She had witnessed her parents persevere in spite of their disrespect for one another and loud fights. Her parents, however, were not telling her to stay in the marriage. They were, in fact, pleading just the opposite because they were deeply worried about their daughter's safety and happiness. Even as parents, they were not welcomed in her home. Bill isolated Susan from them with the explanation that they had botched their responsibilities as parents in her upbringing. Their daughter's inadequacies as a wife, he insisted, were largely the result of their shortcomings. Although they were reluctant to interfere in her marriage, Susan's parents urged her to obtain a divorce.

Susan knew that her stubbornness to make her marriage work made her vulnerable to further abuse. Knowing that she needed to leave the marriage, but that she was unable to, Susan spent three years going to a number of therapists and support groups to understand why. She became caught up in a web of conflicting theories, which fueled the notion that she was having difficulty because something was seriously wrong with her.

Bill was satisfied that Susan was trying to "fix" herself. He himself, of course, made no attempts to improve. He never attended any sessions with his wife. He would sit at home and wait for her return to listen to what insight *she* had attained.

Insight is a tool. We misuse that tool if we expect that once we comprehend *why* we or other individuals behave in a certain manner, then that understanding will have a significant impact upon our lives. Insight alone, no matter how penetrating and accurate, does not forge a new life.

For Susan, reporting to her husband did help to quiet some of his nasty remarks and curb some of his violent outbursts. Susan also felt that searching for some reason for her own behavior temporarily gave her a handle on life. She was disheartened to find, nonetheless, that knowing *why* she functioned in her marriage the way she did was not enough. She still did not know *what* she should be doing about the relationship, or *how* to do it, or *when* to do it.

True insight is formed when you reflect upon what you have experienced in your relationship, arrive at some tentative answers concerning what you need to do, and then test that with additional experience. This is *personal* or *experiential* knowledge.

Intellectual knowledge, in contrast, comes from "thinking about" something. Mentally arranging solutions for and worrying over life's problems, however, do not amend anything. Knowledge that is life-changing can only come from *being in the active process of changing your life.*

We can never fully unravel why we are the way we are. The search for ourselves in past moments of our lives is far less practical and rewarding than the search for ourselves in the very next moment, and then the next moment, and the next . . . .

PAST, PRESENT, FUTURE

Women in violent relationships often feel trapped. A regimen of brainwashing and battering inflicts physical and psychological scars. Loss of control over your body and mind is the sentence imposed upon you by the abuser as punishment for disobedience to his "standards" for a relationship. Any hope for the future seems buried in the outlines of this past. The future looms with sameness, without promise of relief.

Although you feel paralyzed by what you have experienced in the past and are anxious about the future, it is the *present* moment that is the most critical moment in your life. The past and future are of course important. But when you look back at the past, you do so *from the present.* When you imagine your life in the future, you do so again *from the present.*

The only way for you to create a different past is to live well in the present. That is because what you do today becomes, tomorrow, the past. Likewise, the future is fashioned by your actions now. Both the past and the future are linked to each and every thing that you are currently doing and experiencing, routine or extraordinary.

FRESH CHOICES

It may seem that you entertain few choices in your life. The violence you have suffered has effected a sort of myopia concerning the full range of independent actions available to you. Some women arrive at such an extreme state of helplessness that they do not respond to a chance to end the cycle of violence. They have been "manufactured" to feel weak, clumsy, and foolish. Their self-confidence has shriveled from the absence of any meaningful support and the continuous badgering they have received.

Each moment of life, however, does provide a number of options. Each moment is a fresh opportunity. You are not restricted to the consequences of past decisions, for you are processing literally hundreds of choices each day.

There is *always* hope, because significant change can occur at the very next moment. You are not just the victim of *his* moments. He may treat you as a wooden puppet on a string, but you are a person with a voice, a heart, and a soul. Life presents you with your own moments, which only you can fulfill or not.

Once you have accepted the responsibility to choose and act wisely in this and every moment, you begin a new *momentum* for your life.

> *I found that there was a whole world out there without the imposed limits under which I had been suffering. Lots of things were becoming more clear during the days following my decision to leave. I began to live as a healthy, functioning adult. I had been locked in a cage. He had the key. But so did I.*

5 RECYCLING THE PAST

Diaries record the highlights and downswings of our lives. They capture what we may consider too private to disclose to others. The process of selecting experiences and assigning suitable words to them offers a partial release from guarding thoughts and feelings just within ourselves. We can boldly phrase in writing what we may not be able to express aloud. We can commit our concerns to pen and paper even if we cannot tell them to someone who will listen and understand.

READING THE PAST

Diaries are a source of reference by which we are later able to recall our experiences and measure our lives. They detail the manner in which our lives have been constructed. Some of these experiences we may want to forget or deny. But turning the pages of a diary forward is much easier than erasing certain of these experiences from our memory. Recalling the past is always a blend of pleasant remembrance and sobering reminder.

Whether or not we write diaries, the perspective from which we "read" our past is important. It determines if the past remains merely the past or if it is somehow relived and its lessons adopted for the present. The past is unquestionably sealed. What already has occurred is beyond anyone's control to change. What *is* changeable is what we emphasize from the past to influence us now.

> *My mind would drift back and I would cringe. I saw how bizarre my life had been during that time. It amazed me that I could continue under such pressure and still survive. I could clearly see where I had been. After many more months, I actually began to feel thankful that these events had happened to me. I am not saying that I would choose that type of life. The truth is that it was my life and I am a stronger person because of and in spite of what I went through.*

We are never the same person as when we first experienced earlier events. We therefore have the capacity to "recycle" the past by organizing it under new themes. Recycling does not mean that you falsely imagine good where none actually existed. It is finding the good which, in fact, invariably does exist.

Recycling is different than searching the past for some explanation for a current predicament. The attempt to decipher why terrible things happen can cripple you for fear of repeating mistakes and heartaches. To reconsider the past, however, specifically to note the caring, support, and love demonstrated by others, fosters the motivation not simply to survive but to thrive.

> *I think of all the people who talked to me during my marriage. I can now appreciate what they were saying. I was too focused on "poor me" before.*

SOCIAL BALANCE

Living in a violent relationship often produces a twisted view of life and other people. Normal relationships with family, friends, and co-workers are distorted because of the isolation the abuser imposes, the shame you feel about others' finding out about the abuse, or the disintegration of your self-confidence. At times, persons you know or meet may think that you are uncooperative, abrupt, or evasive. They may be puzzled as to some aspects of your behavior or personality. This detachment from others obviously hinders the development of social skills and awareness that other women are experiencing similar life problems.

On the other hand, you may try to compensate for the deficits in your home life by overrelying on your outside relationships. One woman, for example, became understandably empathetic to the plight of other women. She naturally sought their friendship and companionship, but also became highly vulnerable to their demands on her time. They sought her advice and freely gave their own. Although she was flattered, this woman felt an enormous obligation to always be there for her friends. This mutual dependency distracted her from making specific positive changes in her own personal situation.

The correct social balance between our private and public lives is normally fluid. We all have some sense of when we are becoming crowded or intruded upon by others. We also sense when we should be more in their company. Our normal sense, however, is disrupted and blurred by violence. Damaged self-esteem and feelings of powerlessness, when present, do not contribute to seeking out and nurturing healthy relationships. These relationships, however, do not have to await the complete repair of self-esteem or the acquiring of power. All that is needed is the initial willingness and effort to right this social imbalance.

NAIKAN

Mishirabe was the traditional religious practice of a sect of Buddhist priests. For long periods of time these priests would abstain from food, water, and sleep to sit silently and alone in caves to meditate on the condition of their lives. *Naikan* is an adaptation of *Mishirabe* for laypersons whereby the ascetic and spiritual elements have been removed. Meditation has been narrowed and refined to three themes: (1) what was received from significant others in our lives, (2) what was returned to these persons, and (3) what troubles and problems we caused for them. Meditation is still experienced in a quiet setting, frequently a countryside retreat, but with scheduled meals and rest.

Naikan teaches that what we take from others is more than what we give. We insufficiently appreciate and scarcely reciprocate what others, throughout our lives, have done for us. Through week-long meditation on our self-centeredness, with the guidance of a trained instructor, we come to realize that we owe an enormous debt to others. We have received their care in spite of having taken them for granted, or worse, having treated them badly. Everything we are and possess and enjoy originates in the work, generosity, or sacrifice of others. Our pride in the "self-made individual" is based upon a myth. From this realization comes an overwhelming sense of gratitude and the wish to rectify such imbalance through service.

An abuser will convince you that you do not deserve more than what *he* is giving. Reinforced by episodes of violence and periods of "persuasion," *he* insists that *you* are indebted to *him*. The "logic" of an abuser's saying he is doing you a "favor" by exerting forceful control over your life is, of course, not only self-serving but dangerous. Some men do not need the appearance of justification for their abusive behavior. They act according to their own perceived needs or simply by impulse and temper. Other men satisfy any guilt of wrongdoing by calling their actions displays of love or affection.

There is little doubt that the abuser could benefit from *Naikan* meditation, if he were willing to undergo such intensive self-criticism. Properly done, *Naikan* permits little reprieve in its harsh and unrelenting evaluation of how we have treated others, especially those with whom we are most closely related. Unfortunately, many abusers are so invested in finding fault in their spouse or partner, the hope that they would voluntarily submit to any method which seeks to constructively change this attitude may be somewhat wistful and naive.

The goal of changing the abuser must of course be constantly pursued by those in positions to require and monitor that change. In many instances, this means the sanctions and supervision of law enforcement agencies and the courts. It cannot and should not be left simply to the abuser's word that the violence will end. You are entitled to more protection than the string of broken promises that is common among abusers.

Whatever the abuser does or does not do is, however, his responsibility and his alone. He, no one else, exercises control and discretion over his behavior. He therefore must assume the consequences and penalties for his misconduct and violent actions.

NO LONGER A VICTIM

A woman in a violent relationship also is accountable for her own behavior. Every day there are choices to be made. Some of these choices center on just being safe and keeping the pieces of your life together, such as caring for the welfare of your children and juggling finances.

Sadly, there are abusive relationships in which the woman lashes out in retaliation against her husband or boyfriend. Jennifer and Rob both escalated the violence in their relationship until it became a "mutual affray." Whenever he slapped her, she would throw his clothes into the street. Whenever he forced himself upon her in bed, she would puncture one of the tires of his car the next morning. Whenever he yelled at her for being a poor housekeeper, she would hurl a kitchen plate at him. They were locked in a vicious circle of tormenting one another.

You do have the choice of continuing to see yourself as a victim or of beginning to appreciate yourself as a person with a new life ahead. The emphasis of this new life is on what *you can do* rather than on what *he has done to you*. It is turning attention to what *you* need to achieve given the reality of what has already happened in your life. The focus shifts from his violent behavior to your responsibility to give (back) to your life, and to the lives of those you love, what has been taken away by him. One direct way of accomplishing this is to evaluate your life through *Naikan*.

All of us need a deeper appreciation for what we receive from the world around us. This is not a matter of convenience or luxury. It is critical for forming positive relationships with others and a respect for all that exists. For a woman who has suffered a violent relationship, there seems little to appreciate when you are being beaten into submission or your life is a series of crises. Attaining a sense of appreciation, notwithstanding, frees you to involve your life in something other than his abuse.

The whirlpool of his demands and control over you, in other words, weakens as the current of your life becomes stronger.

> *I am not the victim anymore. I know now that I can live in a totally different way. I really must have some incredible inner strength to still have a notion of what is good in life.*

An inflated self-importance and disregard for others is the abuser's profile. Many abusers are convinced that they are society's victims and that *they* deserve better. Although it is absolutely true that you, as a woman in a violent relationship, deserve far better than you are receiving, any improvement in your status must not be at the unfair expense of others. Otherwise, you would mirror the very attitude (of the abuser) that you are endeavoring to leave behind.

6 THE NEXT RELATIONSHIP

The rose has matured from bud to full flower. It is no longer confined to the corner of its existence, but has taken its place in the field of other vibrant flowers. The shadow of its former life remains, but that does not arrest it. Nourished by space, freedom, and the interplay of others, it both gives and receives life.

VULNERABILITY AND READINESS

If you have left an abusive relationship, your life may or may not be suddenly wonderful. The shadow of your past relationship may follow you, not just in recurring memories, but also as you begin to relate to other men. For one area in which the abuser especially controls a woman is her relations with other males. Although some jealousy may exist in even the most secure relationship, the abuser is often exceedingly possessive and vigilant. He interprets your appointments as "rendezvous" and casual acquaintances as "boyfriends." Intimidated by his accusations and attacks, you may have curtailed how and when you related to men.

The abuser, moreover, poisons your perception of men. During courtship you may have been lulled into believing that you had found the perfect mate. There may have been danger signals, but they are only apparent now as you look back. All men are not violent. But the most intimate relationship you have experienced to date has taught you that there are men who can be coarse, domineering, and brutal. Being "owned" by someone as a piece of property, to be "disposed of" at will, is good reason for anger and resentment. How do you trust not only other men—but more important, your own judgment—when it has proven to be so hurtfully wrong?

> *My marriage was very destructive to me. When it was over on paper, I was left with uncertainty about myself and suspicion. For so many years, I was accustomed to assuming that there were double meanings to everything he said. If he said something nice to me, it was because he wanted something. I am still operating out of need to protect myself.*

You cannot prosper when feeling vulnerable and unprotected. Trying to shut out the possibility of all harm, however, may also prevent a healthy relationship with any man. There are no risk-free relationships. There are only relationships in which the couple does or does not mutually accept the risk and does or does not commit to maturing together in the relationship.

You will know when you are ready to accept that risk. As discussed in previous chapters, that readiness is born out of being in touch with your feelings, having some clarity as to your purposes, and building upon the past.

CASTING A NEW RELATIONSHIP

Casting a new relationship supposes some set of ideas concerning the type of relationship you desire. You have already experienced the type of relationship you do *not* want. This does not mean that you therefore know what a fulfilling relationship is.

> *I have a gnawing uncertainty that I will never really be okay again. I want to retreat to my parents' living room and stay there curled up for the next hundred years. I mean, how does one just go on with life after being pushed down stairs, kicked, and humiliated in front of others? How can I think I will be good enough for another person? How do I know what a real relationship is? I am scared. I don't have an answer.*

It is your decision alone whether to enter into another relationship. It is probably best that you neither dismiss that possibility altogether nor rush into finding someone immediately. The emotional wounds from your past relationship will naturally surface periodically. Having been deprived of approval and the security of belonging, you may need the support of family and friends, and other women who have faced similar circumstances before starting a new relationship.

Wounds, however, heal as you strengthen each aspect of yourself. The practice and success gained in one task or project will spill over to other areas.

For example, after her divorce, Cynthia learned to swim underwater in the ocean. She was an average swimmer but had been terrified of diving beneath the surface. This stemmed from her fear of the unknown and not wanting to lose control of her surroundings. A close friend, who was a diver, one day explained to Cynthia that swimming underwater was really the closest thing to flying naturally like a bird that a human being could experience. Suspended in the water, a person could freely glide and harmlessly turn and somersault.

After a few instructions about holding her breath and proper stroking, and accompanied by her friend, Cynthia ventured into the ocean. Outfitted with a snorkel mask, she peered below the surface and felt her usual panic. Her friend dove first and motioned for her to follow. She did, but only succeeded in staying under for a few seconds and only several feet below the surface.

With each subsequent attempt, however, sometimes scurrying to the surface to gasp for air, Cynthia became more and more graceful in her movements. As she became increasingly self-assured, she began to direct her attention away from the mask she had pressed so tightly against her face and away from worries about how far she was from the safety above. She could now marvel at the coral reefs, marine animals, and colorful fish all around her. A whole new world opened up before her eyes.

What Cynthia accomplished was much more than learning how to swim underwater. She found that she could do what she had been so fearful of doing before. She experienced the freedom of attempting something even though the first steps were not perfect. She discovered that where she placed her attention made a great difference in how she viewed life. She had always felt oppressed, claustrophobic, and suffocated in her marriage. Being able to swim underwater was a powerful symbol that she was no longer so confined.

Similarly, as you enter into a new relationship, there will be doubts and fears. But the only thing that guarantees failure is doing nothing. You can, in fact, succeed *even while failing* because success is judged by effort and not by outcome. The outcome depends upon many factors, including the sincerity and endeavor of the other person. You are solely responsible for what *you* bring to the relationship.

EXPECTATIONS

It is important to be realistic in your expectations concerning the new man in your life. This does not mean that you must lower your expectations, but that they must take into account the imperfections in all of us. We all have personality quirks, irritating habits, and noticeable flaws. You may tend to overreact to some of these because your "periscope" is up. As you recognize your own limitations you can identify what effect they have on your present relationship.

> *You become so used to the controls on your life that when there are none, the world seems too much to handle. There is the tendency to find someone who will "take care of everything," who will always be nice. I did meet this man who was*

gentle and affectionate. He actually encouraged me to do my best. A lot of good things were happening because of the relationship, but I was wary. Was this another ploy? It felt right but I held back.

For this woman the psychological scars of her previous relationship were highly visible to her new boyfriend. She had only partially shared with him the true nature of her marriage. He knew it had been abusive but was unclear as to the extent of violence. There were times when he became the undeserving recipient of her rage when she reacted out of painful memories. There were times when she overdepended upon his guidance, and other times that she railed at him for offering any suggestions. She contradicted herself repeatedly as she sought to settle into a safe and comfortable style of relating.

How much should any new man in your life know about your past? At what point should you disclose what you have been through? Certainly if there is danger to him because your former husband or boyfriend will not let you go peacefully, he has a right to know. It will then be his decision about continuing in the relationship. If you both realize that an unpleasant pattern of relating to one another is forming, sorting out the underlying issues may be important.

Honesty about your past relationship, however, does not necessarily require a detailed recitation. The barometer for determining which areas need to be discussed is identifying what purpose it will serve and how it will add to the new relationship. One way to prevent any misunderstanding is to agree on the expectations you each have about revealing one another's past.

BUILDING A PARTNERSHIP

The term "partners" has been defined as "persons who dance with one another, play together in a game against an opposing side, or are close business associates." The emphasis is on cooperation between persons who have joint rights and responsibilities. When couples therefore refer to themselves as partners, the understanding is that all of the above definitions apply.

A healthy relationship must, in other words, address in some measure all aspects of both his and your well-being. For any relationship, there are normal times of smiles, tears, arguments, silliness, excitement, and boredom. The ebb and flow of life does not favor and sustain any particular state but bids us to be alive at each moment and take notice if we are doing our best.

> *I want a partnership. I want pure enjoyment in his company. A special person has walked into my life and I find myself talking and listening with ease. For now, the hardest thing for me is to let love occur naturally. I know that will happen!*

EPILOGUE

There is a saying by Lao-tsu, "Who is there that can make muddy water clear? But if allowed to remain still, it will gradually become clear of itself." In Eastern philosophy, it is from the stillness of this water that the beauty of the lotus flower emerges. It belies its dark surroundings and reaches nobly for the sunlight and skies.

There is no longer the image of a lone feather tenuously positioned over an array of broken eggshells. There is no longer the image of a woman unsure of herself and her future. Strengthened by purpose, engaged in positive activity, and supported by caring others, you begin a new life . . . .

ACKNOWLEDGMENTS

This book was made possible through a grant received from the Department of the Attorney General, State of Hawaii. My appreciation is expressed to The Honorable Warren Price, Laraine Koga, and Earline Yokoi.

The Honorable Joseph Cardoza, prosecuting attorney for the County of Maui; and my staff, Debby Gollehon-Smith, Lena Lorenzo, Jo Lynne Mochizuki, and Rebecca Becker, have provided continuous support.

To Bob Wagstaff and Winnie Yoshikawa-Wagstaff, your artistic talents are greatly admired.

Finally, I have merely gathered in concepts and phrases what has been taught to me by mentors, colleagues, and family, and entrusted to me by those women who have, with courage and resilience, survived and overcome abusive relationships. To these persons, I am grateful for their wisdom, honesty, and patience.

Dr. Brain Ogawa is the Founding Director of the National Academy for Victim Studies and Adjunct Faculty for Victim Issues at the University of North Texas. The Academy is a pioneering program for research, continuing education, instruction and training, and certification in victim services and victimology, and will have a very visible and significant nationwide impact.

Previously, Dr. Ogawa was the Director of Victim/Assistance Division, Department of the Prosecuting Attorney, County of Maui, Hawaii.

In 1995, Dr. Ogawa received the Crime Victim Service Award presented by President Bill Clinton and U.S. Attorney General Janet Reno. He serves on the 1995–96 National Violence Against Women Advisory Council, created by the Department of Justice, and directed by Bonnie Campbell. He also is a consultant and contributing author for the National Crime Victims Agenda, Office for Victims of Crime, U.S. Department of Justice.

His previous books include:

Color of Justice: *Culturally Sensitive Treatment of Minority Crime Victims*
Office of the Governor, Office of Criminal Justice Planning, State of California, 1990

To Tell the Truth
The Children's Museum of Denver, 1993
and
Department of the Prosecuting Attorney, County of Maui, Hawaii, 1988

Volcano Press Titles

Learning to Live Without Violence: *A Handbook for Men* $14.95
by Daniel Jay Sonkin, Ph.D. and Michael Durphy, M.D.

Learning to Live Without Violence: *Worktape* (2 C-60 cassettes) $15.95

The Counselor's Guide to Learning to Live Without Violence $29.95
by Daniel Jay Sonkin, Ph.D., hardcover

Family Violence and Religion: *An Interfaith Resource Guide* $29.95
Compiled by the staff of Volcano Press, hardcover

The Physician's Guide to Domestic Violence: *How to ask* $10.95
the right questions and recognize abuse (another way to save a life)
by Ellen Taliaferro, M.D. and Patricia R. Salber, M.D.

Walking on Eggshells: *Practical Counsel for Women In or Leaving a* $8.95
Violent Relationship by Dr. Brian Ogawa

Every Eighteen Seconds: *A Journey Through Domestic Violence* $8.95
by Nancy Kilgore

Sourcebook for Working With Battered Women by Nancy Kilgore $17.95

Battered Wives by Del Martin $12.95

Menopause, Naturally: *Preparing for the Second Half of Life* $14.95
Updated, by Sadja Greenwood, M.D., M.P.H.

Menopausia Sin Ansiedad $14.95
Spanish edition of *Menopause, Naturally*

Period. by JoAnn Gardner-Loulan, Bonnie Lopez and $9.95
Marcia Quackenbush

La Menstruacion. Spanish edition of *Period.* $9.95

Goddesses by Mayumi Oda $14.95

Lesbian/Woman by Del Martin and Phyllis Lyon, hardcover $25.00

(continued on next page)

Youth and Other Titles from Volcano Press

It's the Law! *A Young Person's Guide to Our Legal System* by Annette Carrel	$12.95
Facilitator's Guide to It's the Law! by Annette Carrel	$16.95
African Animal Tales by Rogerio Andrade Barbosa, illustrated by Cica Fittipaldi, translated by Feliz Guthrie, full color, hardcover	$17.95
Save My Rainforest by Monica Zak, illustrated by Bengt-Arne Runnerström, full color, hardcover	$14.95
Berchick by Esther Silverstein Blanc, illustrated by Tennessee Dixon, hardcover	$14.95
Mother Gave a Shout: *Poems by Women and Girls*, edited by Susanna Steele and Morag Styles, illustrated by Jane Ray, hardcover	$14.95
Mighty Mountain and the Three Strong Women written and illustrated by Irene Hedlund, hardcover	$14.95
Random Kindness & Senseless Acts of Beauty by Anne Herbert and Margaret Pavel with art by Mayumi Oda, accordion-fold, hardcover	$14.95
People of the Noatak by author/artist Claire Fejes	$15.95
Coit Tower: *Its History & Art* by Masha Zakheim Jewett	$10.00

To order directly, please send check or money order for the price of the book(s) plus $4.50 shipping charge for the first book, and $1.00 for each additional book ordered to Volcano Press, P.O. Box 270-40, Volcano, CA 95689-0270, or order by phone with a VISA or MasterCard by calling toll-free 1-800-879-9636. Orders may be faxed to (209) 296-4995.

California residents please add appropriate sales tax.

Volcano Press books are available at quantity discounts for bulk purchases, professional counseling, educational, fund-raising or premium use. Please call or write for details.

✂ ─

☐ Please send a free catalog to:

Name: _____

Address: _____

City, State, Zip: _____

Web Address: http://www.volcanopress.com
Email: sales@volcanopress.com